Your Amazing Itty Bitty™ Awakened Self

15 Key Principles to Self-Awareness

Gina Maron

Published by Itty Bitty™ Publishing
A subsidiary of S & P Productions, Inc.

Copyright © 2024 **Gina Maron**

All rights reserved. No part of this book may be reproduced or transmitted in any form or by any means, electronic or mechanical, including photocopying, recording, or by any information storage and retrieval system, without written permission of the publisher, except for the inclusion of brief quotations in a review.

Printed in the United States of America

Itty Bitty Publishing
311 Main Street, Suite D
El Segundo, CA 90245
(310) 640-8885

ISBN: 978-1-950326-95-2

This book is dedicated to my four remarkable daughters, whose love and unwavering support have been my greatest source of inspiration. Your beauty, both inside and out, shines brightly, and your presence in my life is a constant reminder of the limitless power of love and family.

To all seekers of self-awareness, mindfulness, resilience, and the profound journey of self-discovery, this book is dedicated to you. May these pages serve as a guiding light, igniting your inner wisdom, awakening your spirit, and empowering you to live a life deeply aligned with your heart's true desires. May you embark on a transformative adventure that leads to a new reality, an abundant existence, and the beautiful connection between your heart and mind. Embrace it with courage, trust, and love, for you are on the path to becoming a fully realized being.

In loving gratitude,

Gina, XO

Stop by our Itty Bitty™ website to find interesting blog entries regarding Self-Awareness

www.IttyBittyPublishing.com

Or book a call with Gina Maron at

https://thrivewithgina.com/book-in-a-call/

Unlock the Power With: The Awakened Self

15 Principles to Self-Awareness

The Awakened Self guides you on a transformative journey to discover your true potential and live a life of purpose and fulfillment. Through insightful principles and practical wisdom, this book illuminates the path to self-awareness and inner awakening.

In her Itty Bitty™ book, Gina Maron will help you discover:

- 15 transformative principles to awaken your self-awareness
- Practical exercises to deepen your understanding of each principle
- Insights to navigate challenges and embrace growth
- Tools to harness the power of self-reflection and introspection
- Guidance to align your actions with your deepest values and aspirations

Join the journey to self-discovery and unlock the limitless potential of your awakened self. Your path to empowerment and fulfillment begins here. Pick up a copy of this must-read Itty Bitty™ book today!

Table of Contents

Introduction
- Principle 1. Self-Reflection
- Principle 2. Mindfulness
- Principle 3. Emotional Intelligence
- Principle 4. Values Clarification
- Principle 5. Resilience
- Principle 6. Self-Compassion
- Principle 7. Forgiveness
- Principle 8. Trust
- Principle 9. Curiosity
- Principle 10. Boundaries
- Principle 11. Growth Mindset
- Principle 12. Authenticity
- Principle 13. Vulnerability
- Principle 14. Letting Go
- Principle 15. Receiving

Introduction

Embarking on a journey of self-awareness is the initial step toward transformative change. In the tapestry of life, opportunities abound to create a harmonious existence that aligns with your soul's deepest desires and passions. This book, *Your Amazing Itty Bitty™ Awakened Self, 15 Principles to Self-Awareness,* is your guide to unlocking your authentic self. Inside, you'll discover a wealth of skills and tools, each designed to elevate your consciousness and bring you closer to your higher self. When we feel whole and complete, we resonate with our hearts and minds, creating a life of alignment. Consider this book your compass on the path to self-discovery. You can read it from start to finish, immersing yourself in each principle. Alternatively, select the principles that resonate most with you right now. There's no specific order; the goal is to heighten your self-awareness and illuminate the areas in which you can grow. Your journey to a more profound and authentic self begins here.

Principle 1
Self-Awareness Skills

These five skills begin your journey of self-discovery.

1. The foundation of self-reflection is self-awareness. Start by observing your thoughts, feelings, and behaviors without judgment.
2. Practice being a silent observer of your inner and outer world. This skill enhances your ability to understand the deeper layers of your being.
3. Apply the art of listening to your inner dialogue. Pay attention to the stories you tell yourself. This skill helps to identify unproductive thought patterns.
4. Challenge your beliefs and assumptions. Explore where these beliefs come from and whether these thoughts support your higher self.
5. Self-reflection isn't just about positive feelings; it's about embracing the full spectrum of your emotions. This skill fosters emotional intelligence and resilience.

More About Self-Awareness Skills

Some practices for self-awareness include:

- Exploring where your beliefs come from and whether they serve your authentic self.
- Dedicating a few minutes each day to review your experiences, actions, and feelings.
- Expressing your thoughts and feelings through creativity can provide a unique insight into your inner world.

In the hustle and bustle of daily life, we often forget to pause and look within. As you embark on this transformative journey, you'll find that self-reflection isn't just a tool for understanding yourself; it's the key to unlocking your potential, fostering resilience, and nurturing self-compassion. Self-awareness is your gateway to understanding your thoughts, emotions, and actions at a deeper level.

Principle 2
Mindfulness

These skills introduce you to the essence of mindfulness and its transformative power.

1. Mindfulness begins with paying attention to the here and now. Be fully present in each moment observing your thoughts, emotions, and sensations without judgment.
2. Mindful breathing can be your anchor to the present. Take a few minutes each day to breathe deeply and consciously.
3. Scan your body from head to toe, noticing any tension or discomfort. This practice helps you to become more attuned to your physical sensations.

Mindfulness is the art of being fully present, a practice that transcends meditation into everyday life. These skills can cultivate a more mindful, peaceful, and focused way of living.

More About Mindfulness

By being present in each moment, we can savor life's joys, learn from its challenges, and develop a profound understanding of ourselves. Mindfulness can transform your life in many ways. A few key mindfulness tips are below.

- Mindfulness helps you manage stress by encouraging you to stay present and not dwell on past regrets or future worries.
- It enhances emotional regulation, making you more resilient to life's ups and downs.
- Mindfulness fosters better communication and empathy, enriching your interactions with others.

These bullets connect the concepts of self-awareness and mindfulness, emphasizing how they complement each other.

- Self-awareness is the foundation of mindfulness, helping you identify areas in your life that require deeper presence and awareness.
- Mindfulness enhances self-awareness, allowing you to observe your inner world without judgment.
- Mindfulness is a powerful tool in managing anxiety, depression, and other mental health conditions.

Principle 3
Emotional Intelligence

Each of these skills is like a building block in constructing your emotional intelligence.

1. Developing EQ (Emotional Intelligence) begins with recognizing and acknowledging your own feelings.
2. EQ is about understanding the nuances of your emotions, not just "happy" or "sad," but the subtleties in between.
3. Self-regulation is the art of handling emotional reactions, especially in challenging situations.

By honing these abilities, you can better understand yourself and navigate the complex world of human emotions and relationships.

1. Understanding the feelings of others and building stronger, more meaningful relationships.
2. Developing strong social skills enables you to connect with people on a profound level.
3. Emotional intelligence is the bridge to a more harmonious, authentic, and purpose-driven life.

EQ Tools

- Find an emotional wheel chart to accurately pinpoint and label your emotions. This helps increase your emotional vocabulary and understanding.
- Take a few moments each day to check in with your emotions. Reflect on how you're feeling and why. Write it down in a journal to increase self-awareness.
- Take walks and actively observe the beauty of nature, or simply the world around you while reflecting on things you're grateful for.

Emotional intelligence enhances your self-awareness and empathy, enabling you to navigate relationships and conflicts more effectively.

- EQ builds stronger connections in both your personal and professional life.
- EQ promotes mental well-being, reducing stress and fostering emotional resilience.

As you cultivate these skills and utilize these tools, you embark on a journey of self-discovery and empowerment, where each day is an opportunity to thrive and spread your positive influence in the world.

Principle 4
Value Clarification

Many times what we thought we valued was influenced by external factors, but when we align with our true values, we find fulfillment in our life's journey. Below are soul skills to value.

1. Begin by taking time to reflect on your life and values.
2. Ask yourself what truly matters to you and why.
3. Regularly assess your values by considering how your actions align with your beliefs.

These skills can serve as a foundation for the journey of clarifying and aligning your values with your authentic self.

1. Engage in conversations with your inner self. Listen to your intuition and inner wisdom to discover your true values.
2. When you clarify your core values, you align your life with what truly matters to you.
3. Understanding your values helps you make decisions that are in harmony with your inner beliefs.

Exercises For Value Clarification

Here are some exercises that can help you in the journey of value clarification.

- Find a quiet space, close your eyes, and imagine your ideal life. What values are present in this vision?
- Write down moments in your life when you felt truly fulfilled and satisfied. Analyze these experiences to uncover the values that were present.
- Write down your top five values and describe what each one means to you. This encourages deeper introspection into your values.

Living in line with your values leads to a more satisfying and fulfilling life. You're more likely to find meaning and purpose in your daily experiences.

- Values serve as a source of strength during challenging times. They can help you stay resilient and motivated when facing adversity.
- In essence, clarifying your values is an essential step in the self-discovery journey, as it empowers you to live a more meaningful, purposeful, and authentic life.

Principle 5
Resilience

Resilience is vital on the journey of self-discovery. It equips you to navigate the uncertainties and challenges that arise when you are trying to embrace a new way of living and loving.

1. As you explore new paths and make changes in your life, setbacks are almost inevitable.
2. Resilience gives you the strength to bounce back from setbacks and not be discouraged.
3. Resilience helps you embrace these changes and be adaptable in the face of the unknown. It allows you to see change as a chance to evolve and not as a threat to your stability.

The journey of self-discovery can be uncertain and filled with ambiguity.

1. Embrace adaptability as a skill.
2. Practice breaking down complex issues into manageable parts.
3. Build a strong support network.

Key Elements of a Resilient Mindset

Resilience is the cornerstone of your inner strength.

- Self-efficacy is believing in your ability to influence and control outcomes.
- Optimism is believing that even in difficult situations things can get better.
- Resilient people utilize healthy coping mechanisms such as relaxation, mindfulness, or seeking professional help when dealing with stress.
- Engage in self-care activities that rejuvenate your mind and body.
- Try the 4-7-8 technique: inhale for four seconds, hold for seven, exhale for eight.
- Practice reframing negative thoughts into more positive or constructive ones. This shift in thinking can enhance your problem-solving skills.
- Creating daily routines and schedules can provide structure and stability during challenging times.
- Be kind and understanding toward yourself. Avoid self-criticism and practice self-compassion when facing setbacks.

Embracing resilience on your journey of self-discovery isn't about bouncing back from life's challenges; it's about growing stronger and wiser with each experience.

Principle 6
Self-Compassion

Cultivating self-compassion is crucial for several reasons:

1. It reduces negative self-talk and self-criticism, leading to improved emotional well-being.
2. It helps navigate challenging emotions, such as shame and guilt, with greater ease and kindness.
3. Studies have shown that self-compassion is linked to reduced symptoms of anxiety and depression.

Self-awareness allows you to identify moments of self-criticism or negative self-talk, which are barriers to self-compassion.

1. Treating yourself with the same kindness and understanding that you would offer to a friend is a fundamental skill in self-compassion.
2. Self-compassion also means forgiving yourself for past mistakes and letting go of self-blame.
3. This acceptance of imperfection reduces the pressure to be perfect.

Self-Compassion Is a Skill That Can Be Developed Over Time

Tools for self-compassion:

- Use self-soothing gestures like a self-hug or placing a hand on your heart during moments of distress.
- Use self-compassion mantras: "I am worthy of love and kindness," and, "I am enough just as I am."

The more you engage in these activities, natural self-compassion will become more present in your daily life.

- Keep a small stone or crystal in your pocket. When you touch it, remind yourself to be kind to yourself in moments of self-criticism or stress.
- Practice a body scan meditation where you consciously focus on each part of your body, sending feelings of warmth and love to any areas of tension or discomfort.

As you embark on your journey to self-compassion, remember that within you lies strength, resilience, and untapped potential. Embrace your uniqueness, for it is through your challenges and vulnerabilities that you uncover profound truths about yourself. Self-compassion is the key that unlocks the door to a life filled with kindness, acceptance, and unwavering self-love.

Principle 7
Forgiveness

For significant reasons, forgiveness—especially self-forgiveness—plays a pivotal role when you are on the path of discovering who you are on a soul level.

1. Forgiving others releases the emotional burden of anger, resentment, and grudges.
2. It frees you from carrying negative emotions that can be harmful to your mental and emotional well-being.
3. Forgiveness is an empowering act because it is a choice.

These skills enable you to embark on your journey with an open heart and willingness to learn and grow.

1. Forgiving oneself boosts self-esteem and self-worth.
2. It encourages you to learn from your mistakes and make better choices.
3. Self-forgiveness liberates you from the weight of shame and guilt.
4. It's the key to moving forward with a lighter heart and a sense of renewal.

More About Forgiveness

Forgiveness and self-forgiveness are essential because they clear the path for exploration and self-initiation.

- The journey of self-discovery is often about visiting past wounds, traumas, and mistakes.
- Carrying the weight of unforgiveness, whether directed at yourself or others, can hinder this process.

Practices for forgiveness:

- Imagine releasing the weight of anger or resentment as you let go of a balloon in your mind.
- During meditation, focus on your breath by inhaling self-acceptance and exhaling self-judgment.
- Consider that the person did not intend to hurt you; this can make forgiveness easier.

Without self-forgiveness, you remain tethered to your past, unable to fully embrace the present moment or step into your higher self. By forgiving yourself, you release old burdens, opening the door to profound transformation and the opportunity to create a life aligned with your deepest authentic values. It's a crucial step on your journey toward self-discovery and conscious evolution.

Principle 8
Trust

Trust is fundamental to your soul's journey of becoming whole and embracing your divine nature within a human experience. Here are six skills to support this principle:

1. Begin by trusting yourself. Listen to your intuition and inner wisdom.
2. Believe that the universe has a divine plan for you.
3. Open your heart to others and allow vulnerability.

Trust is your anchor, the unwavering belief that you can navigate change and uncertainty with resilience and grace.

1. Understand that every step in your journey serves a purpose.
2. Trust that even difficulties have meaning and lead you to your higher self.
3. Be patient and trust that things will unfold in their own time.

More About Trust

By nurturing self-trust, you gain the confidence to embrace your authentic self and all the beauty it holds. Believe in your intuition, honor your abilities, and remember that you are a spiritual being having a human experience. Try the following self-trust exercises.

- Keep a journal of past accomplishments, both big and small. This reinforces your belief in your capabilities.
- Whenever you have a gut feeling or intuitive insight, act on it.

When you deepen your self-trust, you'll find your path will be clearer, your purpose more profound, and your journey more meaningful.

- Observe the harmony and balance in the natural world. This helps you trust in the order of the universe.
- Practice letting go of the need to control outcomes and trust that things will unfold as they should.
- Every day see yourself as confident, empowered, and trust your own decisions.

As you nurture self-trust through these exercises, you'll uncover the incredible strength residing within you. Trust yourself and embrace the profound journey of conscious evolution and a life aligned with your deepest calling.

Principle 9
Curiosity

When you approach life with curiosity, you remain open to possibilities and receptive to learning.

1. Curiosity invites you to question the status quo, challenge your beliefs, and deepen your understanding of yourself.
2. Embrace curiosity and you'll embark on a journey of discovery that enriches your human experience and expands your consciousness.

Ignite curiosity with the following ideas.

1. Practice asking yourself open-ended questions like, "What if?" or, "Why not?"
2. Be open to exploring new ideas, experiences, and places. It's in the exploration of the unknown that curiosity thrives.
3. Observe the world with fresh eyes, as if you are seeing it for the first time.

Exercises to Initiate Curiosity

- Try your hand at various creative endeavors like writing, painting, or playing a musical instrument.
- Keep a journal next to your bed to write down your dreams.
- Analyzing your dreams can lead to curious insights about your subconscious.
- Select an object like a flower and take a moment to closely observe it. Focus on the small details you might otherwise miss.
- Commit to learning something new every day, no matter how small.
- Spend time with children and observe their natural curiosity and sense of wonder.

Embrace your curiosity; it is the guiding star of your soul's journey. As you venture into the uncharted realms of your inner world, remember that curiosity is the compass that leads to the profound revelations and transformations that await.

Principle 10
Establishing Healthy Boundaries

Here are a few skills that support healthy boundaries.

1. Learning to value and respect yourself is the foundation of setting and maintaining healthy boundaries.
2. Know that it is perfectly acceptable to decline things that don't align with your values and well-being.
3. Learn to express your needs, desires, and limits clearly and assertively.

Healthy boundaries promote self-respect, reduce stress, and nurture positive connections.

1. Develop conflict resolution skills to constructively address boundary violations and disagreements.
2. Practice mindfulness to stay present and attuned to your feelings and needs.
3. Prioritize self-care as a non-negotiable part of your routine.

Mastering healthy boundaries and self-honoring acts will bring you the gift of inner peace and self-respect.

Self-Honoring Acts

These exercises can help you develop and maintain healthy boundaries.

- Spend a few minutes each day reflecting on your feelings and needs.
- Are there any emotions you need to address or boundaries to reinforce?

Understanding what's truly important to you can help you set boundaries that align with your authentic self.

- Reflect on your core values and beliefs.
- Keep a journal to record your thoughts, emotions, and boundary-setting process.

Embracing healthy boundaries empowers you to reclaim your inner balance and live a life true to your values. As you integrate these skills into your journey of self-discovery, you'll discover newfound freedom, deeper connections, and a profound sense of self-love.

It is through boundaries that you truly honor yourself and create the life you deserve. Step into your full potential as a conscious, awakened being.

Principle 11
Growth Mindset

The following skills support your expansion and grow your mindset.

1. View challenges as opportunities for growth rather than threats.
2. Cultivate a mindset that welcomes difficulty as a chance to learn and improve.

With a growth mindset, you're more likely to embrace challenges, persevere through obstacles, and learn from your experiences.

1. Rather than fearing mistakes, consider them valuable lessons.
2. Be open to constructive feedback.
3. Welcome change and adaptation, two key aspects of conscious evolution.

A growth mindset opens doors to self-discovery and an evolved state of consciousness to foster continuous expansion of your horizons, deepening of your self-awareness, and striving to reach your fullest potential.

Tools to Build and Strengthen Your Mind

- Regularly do something that takes you out of your comfort zone.
- Embrace discomfort as a chance for growth.
- When you catch yourself using limiting language or self-criticism, reframe your thoughts with a positive twist.

Set goals that focus on personal development, not just outcomes.

- Vividly visualize your goals and future successes.
- See yourself achieving what you desire.
- When faced with problems or obstacles, focus on finding a solution rather than dwelling on the issue.

Embrace the growth mindset and you'll discover the power of continuous transformation. With each challenge, you'll recognize an opportunity for growth, and in every step of your journey, you will find the path to your most extraordinary self. Your growth mindset is the key to unlocking a life of boundless possibilities.

Principle 12
Body Intelligence

Body intelligence matters because the body often reacts physically in response to emotions. By paying attention to bodily sensations, you can gain deeper insight into your emotional world. The body often provides early signals or "gut feelings" about situations. Trusting your instincts can lead to wiser decisions and a deeper connections to your life's purpose.

1. Acknowledging the relationship between body and mind can help you address stress and trauma, ultimately leading to healing and personal growth.
2. Your body holds memories at both a conscious and subconscious level.
3. Use it as a guide, a repository of memories and wisdom, and a conduit to greater understanding.

As you develop these skills, you can tap into your innate intelligence.

More About Body Intelligence

Using movement to explore your body's memory and emotional responses can be a powerful tool for healing and self-discovery. Here is how to tune in:

- Through deep, intentional breathing during movement, you can bring awareness to your emotional state.
- Close your eyes and take deep breaths. As you inhale, imagine drawing energy up from the Earth to your core. As you exhale, release any tension or negative emotion.
- Dancing freely with intention to music can be a powerful way to express your emotions and connect with your inner self.
- While walking slowly focus on your breath, your surroundings, and the sensations in your body.
- Don't shy away from discomfort during movement. Lean into it gently, as this is where emotions may surface. Through the rhythmic movements of your body and the stillness of your mind, you uncover the boundless treasures within, weaving a tapestry of wholeness, bringing deep healing, and awakening your fullest potential.

Principle 13
Vulnerability

Vulnerability is the courageous act of unveiling our true selves to the world. Here are some qualities of vulnerability:

1. Openness
2. Willingness to learn
3. Empathy
4. Self-acceptance
5. Healthy boundaries
6. Resilience
7. Authenticity
8. Emotional awareness
9. Trust and courage
10. Valuing human connection

These characteristics are powerful and transformative qualities. When you're vulnerable, you open and share your truths, even the painful ones. Helping you release baggage associated with old stories, releasing old stories creates space for new beginnings to unfold.

More about Vulnerability

Remember that vulnerability is a courageous act of self-expression, and it's a journey. Take small steps and be patient with yourself.

- Opening up to someone you trust is a powerful way to practice vulnerability.
- Creative expression can help you tap into your emotions and vulnerabilities.
- Take time to reflect on your life journey, your strengths, and your weaknesses.
- Take some time to write down your fears, no matter how small or large.
- This practice can help you become more aware of what you're holding back and what vulnerabilities you're guarding.
- If you're struggling to open up and practice vulnerability, consider seeking help from a therapist or a counselor.

Vulnerability is the key that unlocks the door to profound self-discovery, a journey where you can break free from emotional barriers and fears. As you courageously embrace your true self, you invite authenticity into your life. Deepening your connection with your inner being and those around you.

Embrace your vulnerability; it's the birthplace of strength and transformation.

Principle 14
Letting Go

Surrender is the key to self-discovery. Here are some insights to let go and surrender to what is.

1. They allow you to release the grip of preconceived notions and expectations.
2. They enable you to free yourself from the burden of attachments.
3. Surrender is the key to self-discovery, spiritual growth, and living your life rooted in the present moment.

Here are a few skills to support your journey:

1. Cultivating mindfulness helps you become aware of your attachments and resistance.
2. Accept things as they are without the need to control and change them.
3. Write down what you want to release and then burn the paper.

More About Letting Go

By releasing old patterns, beliefs, and attachments you create room for personal growth. Sometimes the most profound moments occur when you let life take you where it wants to go.

- Letting go paves the way for healing, transformation, and a more fulfilling life.
- Letting go opens space for new experiences, relationships, and opportunities.
- Releasing attachments to past mistakes or regrets fosters self-acceptance.

Surrender is a journey, not a destination. Here are some tools to support the process:

- Are you attached to, an outcome, a material possession, or a relationship?
- Life has its own rhythm; trust that things will work out as they are meant to.
- Meditation can connect to your inner self and higher guidance.
- Listen to your inner voice. Let intuition guide you to the right path.

In the dance of life, surrender is the graceful step leading you to your higher self and the universe. As you release the need for control, you'll find what surrounds the doorway to self-acceptance.

Principle 15
Receiving

Embrace the art of receiving as a sacred dance with the universe, where your soul aligns with the abundant offerings of life.

1. Learn to say yes to receiving.
2. Sometimes it's as simple as being willing to accept help, love, or opportunities that come your way.
3. Have faith that life provides you with what you need when you need it.
4. Spending time in nature allows you to receive its wisdom, peace, and serenity.

Your journey unfolds as you learn to receive with an open heart.

1. Being kind to others fosters a giving-receiving cycle.
2. In your meditation practice, focus on receiving positive energy and letting go of resistance.

Practices to Enhance Receiving

- During interactions with others, be fully present and engaged.
- Listen actively and acknowledge the generosity of others.
- Self-nurturing helps you build self-worth and a sense of deserving.
- Affirmation: "I am open to receiving all the blessings the universe is gifting me."
- Contemplate your beliefs on receiving and see if they are limiting you.

Receiving creates balance in the giving and taking cycle of life. When we receive, we align with the natural ebb and flow of the universe, which promotes harmony and equilibrium.

- Being receptive means, you are open to life's experiences, lessons, and opportunities.
- When you are receptive you're willing to change and adapt to new experiences.
- Receiving links you to a higher power or your inner self, offering profound gifts.

Embrace the art of receiving and you'll embark on a journey of self-discovery that leads to deeper connections, greater abundance, and a richer, more fulfilling life.

You've finished. Before you go...

Post/Share that you finished this book.

Please star rate this book.

Reviews are solid gold to writers. Please take a few minutes to give us some itty bitty feedback.

ABOUT THE AUTHOR

Gina Maron is a seasoned and compassionate coach dedicated to assisting individuals in overcoming their challenges and igniting transformational change. Her journey has been deeply personal, marked by understanding what it means to feel trapped, disconnected, and disempowered. Her quest for answers and healing led her on a path of profound self-discovery and personal growth.

After entering into a marriage and family life, Gina realized that external success did not necessarily equate to inner fulfillment. This realization sparked her journey of deep soul searching. Gina explored various modalities, delved into the study of spiritual psychology, and sought wisdom from mentors and teachers. Along this path, she honed the extraordinary power of self-love and acceptance, committing herself to sharing these insights and tools with others.

With over a decade of coaching experience, Gina has guided numerous individuals on their own transformative journeys. Her approach is distinctive, drawing from spiritual psychology, embodiment practices, and intuitive guidance. This unique blend enables her to forge profound connections with her clients, guiding them toward inner healing and empowerment. At the heart of her practice is the creation of a safe and nurturing space, where individuals can delve into their inner worlds, heal past wounds, and step into their true potential.

Gina's expertise extends beyond coaching. She is a Harvard graduate holding a master's degree in spiritual psychology, with a specialization in conscious health and healing. Furthermore, she is a Kundalini yoga teacher, sound healer, and mother of four amazing daughters. Her forthcoming book, *Home Frequency,* set to be published next year, offers additional insights and tools for personal transformation.

Through her podcast, *All About You,* Gina has had the privilege of featuring renowned healers and practitioners, expanding her knowledge, and sharing invaluable insights with her audience.

Gina's wealth of experience continues to make a significant impact in the lives of those she coaches, helping them cultivate a profound sense of peace, harmony, and happiness within.

If you enjoyed this Itty Bitty™ book you might also like…

- **Your Amazing Itty Bitty™ Relationships As A Spiritual Practice** by Deborah A. Gayle

- **Your Amazing Itty Bitty™ Aging Well Book** by Michele McHenry

- **Your Amazing Itty Bitty™ Intuitive Hypnosis Book** by Saba Hocek

Or any of the many Amazing Itty Bitty™ books available online at www.ittybittypublishing.com

www.ingramcontent.com/pod-product-compliance
Lightning Source LLC
Chambersburg PA
CBHW061305040426
42444CB00010B/2531